GW00686222

THE NITPICKING OF CRANES

PADDY BUSHE

THE DEDALUS PRESS

IRISH CANCER SOCIETY
69 LR.CAMDEN STREET,DUBLIN 2.

DATE 16/08/2024 FRI TIME 16:54

BOOKS   €1.00
TOTAL   €1.00
CHARGE1   €1.00

CLERK 1   242336   00001

Paddy Bushe

o

The Nitpicking of Cranes

o

DEDALUS

The Dedalus Press
24 The Heath ~ Cypress Downs ~ Dublin 6W
Ireland

© Paddy Bushe and The Dedalus Press 2004

ISBN 1 904556 31 0 paper
ISBN 1 904556 32 9 bound

Some of these poems, or versions of them, were published in the following periodicals: *Agenda, The Amethyst Review, Black Mountain Review, Books Ireland, The Burning Bush, Fire, Kotaz, Magma, Merseyside Arts Monthly, Metre, New Orphic Review, Orbis, Other Poetry, Paris-Atlantic, The Sewanee Review, The Shop, Southword, South, The Word.*
Most of the poems in Irish have been published in *In Ainneoin na gCloch* (Coiscéim, 2001). All translations of the poems from the original Irish are by the author
The author is especially grateful to An Chomhairle Ealíon, The Arts Council, for a bursary which enabled him to work on this collection.

Cover Painting by Zhang Xiang

The Dedalus Press is represented and distributed in the U.S.A. and Canada by **Dufour Editions Ltd.**, P.O. Box 7, Chester Springs, Pennsylvania 19425
in the UK by **Central Books**, 99 Wallis Road, London E9 5LN

The Dedalus Press receives financial assistance from
An Chomhairle Ealaíon, The Arts Council, Ireland.
Printed in Dublin by Johnswood Press

for Fiona, my heart's travelling companion

Stamp
for Zhang Xiang

You carved my own seal for me, your chisel
Discovering in marble new characters for my name,
Endowing its plain syllables with *learning* and *inspiration.*

I coax these words on to a blank page,
Sending them with gratitude to the east,
Stamped with my new characters in crimson ink.

Contents

7

three

One

John Donne in Beijing

Conceits flew right out the taxi window
Into the blare of traffic, the muggy
High-pitched, buying and selling streets.
My mind, agape, circled and reeled
Like a compass staggering across the globe
Or a drunk repeating and repeating
Hall of Divine Harmony, Temple of Buddhist Fragrance,
Stone Staircase of Auspicious Clouds.

Later, in the hotel, while the television
In the background showed Chinese opera,
Drone and whine pitched themselves into sweetness
As we opened and closed ourselves like a fan
And made that little room an everywhere,
Our own small *Palace of Immortality.*

Canal Buddha

Bougainvillea and dozens of anonymous
Creepers trailed towards the water
From every stilted house and balcony,
As our long-tailed, long-nosed boat
Probed the backwaters of Bangkok's canals.
At house after house I photographed
Miniature temples, layered and decorated
With tiny Buddhas and all due ceremony.

Suddenly, as we floated by yet another one,
Draped with yellow scarves and lotus blossoms,
I thought I heard, in a faraway accent,
A blessing, thick-tongued yet familiar:
Kavanagh, serendipitous in a *stupa*,
A canal-bank shrine for the passer-by.

Blithe Newcomers

Just a day or two in Korea, and still
Jetlagged, trying to orientate ourselves,
We take the mountain path, marvelling
At the calligraphy, among strange trees,
Of butterflies, jet-black, as big as wrens.

Suddenly, as we reach the summit
And all the wooded peaks rise and roll
Horizon beyond horizon to the east,
A familiar, wandering voice, reincarnated,
Transliterating perfectly: *kŭ'ku, kŭ'ku.*

Advice for a Poet

In Yuantong Temple, the signs
In translation speak in auspicious tones.

Near a cloistered pool, smiled upon
By statues gilded with serenity,

I am urged to *avoid conflagration*,
And to *offer incense with civility*.

Above all, a sign beseeches me,
Please make no confused noise while chanting.

The Poet of the Terraces Remembers

Like nomadic herdsmen, I had thought, they would come
And go, in skin robes and broad-brimmed hats,
With daggers at their multicoloured belts.

I had imagined the sound of hooves and bells
Addressing urgencies of clouds and seasons,
Of distant grasslands and snow on the high passes.

And in summer, I had thought, they would return
At a gallop, whooping for a festival
With rounds of wild dances, and of stories.

But they came, my poems, like farmers
Doggedly each day along the same paths
Between terraces, hoes on their shoulders.

They bent their backs, scraped and groped
For days and months until they harvested
The sweetest grains, berries that held the light.

And they went each night to the herdsmen's fires
Danced, heard stories, and traded their harvest
For wide-horned cattle, sleek from the grasslands.

Wine-Cup

At Kyonju, beside the tiny stream
Shaped by cut granite to the outline
Of an abalone-shell, I conjure once again
A ceremonial of poets and calligraphers.

From the pavilion I conjure lacquered tables,
Ink-sticks of soot pressed with camphor,
Porcelain brush-pots, silk and layered paper.
Squirrels and moths are flitting in attendance.

I conjure the most venerable among us
To place a brimming wine-cup,
Glazed by candles and moonlight,
Into the exact centre of the stream.

Whenever it grounds itself against the bank,
Like a line that has faltered, the nearest one
Must rescue it, drink and compose there and then
Words for the company, characters for the page,

Then fill and float it away again. I wait
As it circles around and around the rim
Of the shell, nodding graciously each time
It passes me, away beyond my conjuring.

Frog Song

Spring. In the flooded paddies
Rice stalks shoot fresh green
From their own reflections.

I walk along narrow ridges
Between paddies. Paths dip
Into sod walls and out again.

My stretched arms bank
Left and right, hold me
In exquisite balance.

The air is pulsing with frogs,
All of them on the one note:
Basho ...Basho ...Basho ...

An Mhuintir agus an Éigse
do Ba Da Chai

De thaisme, más ann in aon chor dá leithéid,
A bhuaileamar, mise ar shiúlóid maidne,
Tusa ag dúnadh dorais. *This my study house.*
What do you study? Make poems. So do I!
Agus away linn díreach go dtí an scoil filíochta agat
(*Peoples and Poems* a d'aistrís an t-ainm le scairt)
Ar bhruach an chuain. Seomra geal, fairsing,
Boird agus mataí ina n-áiteanna féin,
Agus druma mór chun rithime ar an urlár

B'fhada fada sinn ó sheomraí dorcha
Agus clocha ar bhrollach gach ábhar file.
Gach aon fhuinneog níos niamhraí ná a chéile:
Sliogiascairí i gcrithloinnir an lagtrá,
Nóra na bPortach agus éirí-níos-airde uirthi
Leis an gclúmh geal bán a fuair sí anseo timpeall,
Agus Ilch'ubong, Mullach Éirí na Gréine,
Ag taibhreamh ar thine a spalpadh amach arís
Ach an lá a bheith róbhrothallach.

Mhalairtíomar leabhair go deasghnáthúil
Agus d'ólamar té glas go deasghnáthúil,
(Agus ba dheas, gnáthúil mar a dheineamar)
Inár suí go ciarógach ag bord íseal,
Ag tabhairt aitheantas cuí dá chéile.
Agus cé gur bhrathas ar dtús iartharach, tuathalach,
Fiú corrthónach, d'éiríos diaidh ar ndiaidh
Suaimhneach, oirthearach, (Searcenstockach, dá ndéarfainn é)
In Songsan, i dtigh geal sin na filíochta.

Peoples and Poems
for Ba Da Chai

It was by chance, if there is any such thing,
That we met, me out for a morning walk,
You closing a front door. *This my study house.*
What do you study? Make poems. So do I!
And away with us to your school of poetry
(*Peoples and Poems,* you translated the name, laughing)
On the edge of the sea. A lucent, airy room,
Tables and floor-mats, each in its own space,
And a skin drum invoking rhythm on the floor.

We were miles and miles from darkened rooms
And bardic apprentices with stones on their chests.
Each window framed more magic than the next:
Shellfish-gatherers in the shimmering ebb-tide,
Nora the Heron getting even more stuck-up
With the white crane's outfit she picked up around here,
And Ilch'ubong, the Summit of the Rising Sun,
Dreaming about erupting one more time,
Only that the day was far too warm.

We exchanged books ceremoniously
And drank green tea, again ceremoniously,
(And the ceremony was marvellously everyday)
As we sat cross-legged at a low table,
Eyeing each other with due recognition,
And although I was awkward and western,
You could even say tight-arsed, I became inch by inch
Easier, more oriental, (dare I say Searcenstockian?)
In Songsan, in that luminous house of poetry.

Crossing Waibaidu Bridge
for Zhang Ye

The moon has suspended your poem over the bridge
And sharpened the bite of the wind off the river.

Long convoys of barges, bow nudging stern,
Are buffeting their dogged way against the current.

I do not know what cargoes they carry,
Or how far up the river they will travel.

Nor do I know anything of your burdens,
The distances you have travelled, or will.

But I think you have bowed to the stern buffeting
Of your life's currents, yet still held your buoyancy.

When this bridge first spanned the river in wood,
It demanded a toll from everyone who crossed.

Now that steel has arched itself into its bones,
Waibaidu exacts no price from those who cross over.

And though you must hold fast to the steel in your mind,
May green sap always rise to blossom in your soul.

(The name Waibaidu signifies that no toll need be paid.)

Petals

for Philip Casey

The waitress placed a vase of grassland flowers
On the table where I was reading *The Water Star*.
Hesitant, practising English, she asked its name,
Then frowned at my phrasebook's characters.
Shui Xing? ..... But, in water, is no star.

As I mimed reflection, pointing to huge distances,
Her eyes lit with sudden understanding
And she laughed with delight at the image.
I turned again, smiling, to my book.
Two petals shimmered on the open page.

Zhongdian, 6 July 2000.

Tread Softly

I had thought she was only my dream,
The Naxi woman who paused at dawn
On the stone bridge in Lijiang.

But I saw the light touch, on her shawl,
The silver thread of the seven circles
Worn as reflections of sun, moon and stars.

So I, being rich, bring back and spread
Before your waking, wondering eyes
This fragment of the heavens' embroidered cloths.

Afternoon in Kunming

In Green Lake Park, the afternoon crowd
Gathering in and around the pavilion

Was mostly pensioners, old comrades in cards,
Settling companionably near the music.

When the younger woman was called,
She spat to clear her throat before pitching

Her voice so perfectly to the bamboo flute
That applause almost drowned her singing.

And when she danced whatever story
Flowed between the *erhu* and the bells,

Her rayon blouse and fat, miniskirted legs
Liquified themselves into the music,

As cranes might pick their white, reflected way
Dreamily through the mud of patterned terrraces.

I saw the lined, watching faces lift up and shine
Like dry bamboo absorbing morning sun.

Morning on the Night Train

Dawn. The train coughs and splutters,
Taking water at a small, empty station

In the gorge that snakes its dry way
Through the crumbling plateau of Gansu.

Light seeps down the cliffs, gilds
The corrugated iron of the sheds.

When I slide open a window, releasing
Smoke and food smells into the thin air,

Birdsong, something like a thrush,
Overflowing with rise and ripple,

Begins to sprinkle itself on the morning.
A window slides in the next carriage

And eager lips and tongue and throat
Whistle out a stream of perfect mimicry.

I'd swear those bubbling voices join
To pitch themselves up to the still

Wide-eyed stars, charming them
One by one into a dreamless sleep.

Music Lesson, Xiahe

I remember it still, the young monk's delight
At the chance meeting with us on the hill,
The phrase-book hauled from the depths of his robe

Redolent of drawing-rooms and radiantly
Enthusiastic about self-improvement.
He opened it at random, and between

Introductions and *The Rules of Tennis,*
It offered, in English, Tibetan and Chinese,
The vocabulary of *Playing the Piano.*

You both pulled out imaginary stools
And, exquisitely occidental, he read
Would you be so kind as to turn the pages?

He tinkled and jangled the strange consonants
Around his tongue, applauding the right notes,
While arpeggios of giggles accompanied mistakes.

And as he fingered the unfamiliar keys,
The *basso profundo* of the huge monastery trumpets
Reverberated up the hill, and the great gong

On the roof-top brazenly imposed a silence
That would become the world's one note
In the fragrant, chanting halls below.

And to his *do you find the music pleasant?*
The phrase-book prompted you: *simply delightful!*
And it was. And it echoes. Still.

Dawn Notes

At six exactly, the first, tentative bird
Trebles in the morning from the courtyard,
Pines and bamboo stirring to the sound.

Tile by tile, the curves of neighbouring roofs
Lilt themselves into the sky, and the bugle
From the barracks next door blows

The remains of the night fog away.
A bus hoots past a woman yoked
To two baskets for the market.

The night watchman on his mattress
Hawks and spits himself awake,
Smiles, and singsongs me good morning.

Yangshuo River Walk

for Qin Jiang Rong

My rolls of film, now developed, scroll
Down that drizzling day again, the river
Unwinding itself between pinnacles
Draped exquisitely over themselves.

Bamboos drooping with mist crisscross
As we crisscrossed the river between villages
Dirt poor among rich orchards, rice paddies
And *sweet potatoes only for the festival.*

Once again I am being ink-brushed
Into a landscape more insubstantial
Than the mist where it is cocooned.
I am complicit in my own disappearance.

But the mud of that river walk clings
In my memory as it clung to my boots,
And I still taste the pomelo whose seeds
We spat in circles of laughing around us,

As the cruise-boats on the river klaxoned,
And you recited Li Bai, so that I heard
For the first time the pattern and rhyme
Of his loneliness and moonlit exile.

I put the photographs away in the drawer
Of my imagination. The gloss changes,
Begins to spin itself into a silk scroll,
Unwinding as my pen becomes a brush.

The Poet Pines in Exile in Suzhou

The neon sky is sodden with mist tonight,
Discoloured as the canals that carry
Plastic bags under stepped stone bridges
In ornamental gardens. Here scribes and poets
Wrote elegantly of absent friends and distant wives.

Leaves that should compose their own calligraphy
Of loneliness under a clarifying moon
Are limp in its absence. Even poor Li Bai
Had his own shadow to keep him company
And with him raise a wine-cup to the moon.

My shadow lies within myself. And so
I spin a globe and from that shadow
I create a moon. I imagine its clear
Fullness over Binn Mhór, the touch of frost
That makes you settle deeper in our bed.

Dorchadas

An dorchadas is doimhne amuigh
Is ea an duibheagán istigh
Nuair a thuislíonn sé as cúl a chinn
Amach faoin tsolas gan trua.

Van Gogh, abair, nuair a ghread
Préacháin thuarúla a aigne
Amach os cionn ór cruithneachta
Agus gile uafásach a scuaibe.

Nó Li Bai, a báthadh sa Yangtse,
I measc tuillte focal agus fíona,
Ag iarraidh an bharróg ba bharrógaí amuigh
A bhreith ar an ngealach ins an uisce.

Darkness

The deepest darkness in the wide earthly world
Is the blackness within
When it staggers from the back of the mind
Out into the relentless light.

Van Gogh, say, when the ominous
Crows of his imagination
Flew up over the golden wheat
And the terrible brightness of his brush.

Or Li Bai, drowned in the Yangtse
In floods of words and wine,
Trying to embrace the wide earthly world
Of the moon reflected in water.

Li Bai's Last Poem

(Li Bai, the great poet of the Tang dynasty, is said to have drowned while drunkely trying to embrace the moon's re flection in a lake)

I

The more my boat rocks, the more
Exuberantly the moon disports itself
Among the ripples. I dip my oars

Into one shining facet or another
Of that reflected light, and I zig
And zag somehow to the lake's centre

And spin myself to a shaky stop.
On the shore, a lantern flickers.
I can hear the cry of my peacock

Bounce itself from star to brittle star
And rattle into silence. I uncork
My wine-jug and ceremoniously pour

A measure for myself and a measure
Ceremoniously, as always, for another.

II

All of my life has been other, is absence:
Farewells in wine-shops, Meng Haoran's sail
Diminishing down the length of the Yangtse,

Poems to and from Du Fu, their characters
Like heads bowed in exile, like wild geese
Crossing a cold moon above bare branches.

All those merchants' wives, those distant
Administrators yearning for their families,
Were versions of myself, listening

Desperately for footsteps along the path,
Searching the Milky Way for friends,
Combing the wind for the hermit's flute,

Raising a wine-cup, a jolly good fellow,
Cavorting with the moon and my own shadow.

III
Another cup of wine. The shadowed
Mountains across the lake are watching
Like judges in their long dark robes.

Lighten yourselves! I do not threaten
The order of the state. Let the record show
That even I — yes I! — was once tempted

By imperial affairs: a court academy,
No less, of compliant poets, commissioned
To spin line after silken line of flattery,

While an emperor searched for immortality
In elixirs, or the arms of Yang Guifei. I sang
One or another's praise. For a time, it trapped me.

Listen, moon! That fool of a man, his concubine,
Are less to me now than this cup of wine.

IV

Place, too, becomes a kind of absence
For the wanderer. Even after sixty years
I can still pine for the distant grasslands

Of my childhood, their huge perspectives
Along flowered valleys to the high passes,
The tents, the cattle-bells, the whooping herdsmen.

My breath still catches on the pine-incensed road
Into Sichuan. I sigh day after day for fishermen
Poling bamboo rafts on the river at Yangshuo,

And my heart still scales the hundred terraces
Of Dragon's Back Mountain, where white cranes
Walk in a dream, entranced by their own elegance.

Agh, more wine! The traveller's curse
Is to ache to be everywhere, all at once.

V

No more wine. I fling the empty jug
Through space at the moon's reflection
With the rage of a lover whose love

Has turned bitter. The image breaks
Into a thousand slivers that pierce
My eyes, my heart, then turn to flay

Me alive. Alive? There are ways to be alive:
In peach blossoms in spring, in the flow
And flood of the Yangtse, in those high

Stripped places where I must journey soon,
Never again to raise a parting wine-cup.
In the lake's mirror, the shining moon,

That just now I shattered, is shaking
Itself whole again. I must embrace it.

Two

Rice Terraces

The watered and stone-lined
Terraces pattern the hills,
Ascending and descending

As regularly as the decorous
And predetermined steps
Of a Confucian argument.

The bright new shoots
Seem to rise from a sky
Whose cloudless reflections

Are disturbed only rarely
By the slow, fastidious
Nitpicking of cranes.

Ag Aistriú *Buddha in Der Glorie*

In aghaidh mo thola, bhí sé caite uaim agam,
An smaoineamh go n-aistreoinn an dán sin le Rilke,
Cé go raibh sé fillte agus aithfhillte trím aigne
Mar a bheadh bratóg urnaithe ar chrann naofa.

Fuaireas róchoimhthíoch iad, na críocha úd
Ina raibh an dán agus an t-aistriúchán ag taisteal,
An ghramadach débhríoch, agus nósmhaireacht an táirsigh
Suite mar chonstaic ar mo chead isteach.

Ach nuair a bhaineas mo bhróga iartharacha díom
Roimh gabháil thar táirseach Teampall Phrah Singh,
Is nuair a shuíos croschosach ag análú tiúise,
Cloigíní ag bualadh i leoithne anseo is ansiúd,

D'aithníos Búda Rilke os mo chomhair in airde,
Ceannbhrat naoi gciseal go caithréimeach
Ar foluain os a chionn. I loinnir an íomhá,
Thuigeas go bhféadfaí go ndéanfaí teanga díom.

Translating *Buddha in Der Glorie*

Against my will, I had put to one side
The notion of translating that poem by Rilke,
Although it had wound itself around my mind
Like a prayer-flag around a holy tree.

They were too alien to me, those regions
Where poem and translation were travelling;
The grammar ambiguous, and the threshold customs
Squatting like guardians against my entering.

But when I took off my Western shoes
Before crossing the threshold of Wat Phrah Singh,
And when I sat, cross-legged, breathing incense,
Temple bells tinkling somewhere in the breeze,

I recognised Rilke's Buddha high up before me,
A nine-tiered canopy floating triumphantly
Above his head. In that resplendent image
Gleamed all the possibilities of all language.

Búda faoi Ghlóir

Croí gach chroí, lár gach láir,
Cnó laistigh de féin ag milsiú,
Cruinne na réalt is sia ar fad siar
Is ea toradh d'ioncholluithe: soraidh chugat.

Féach anois nach bhfuil ceangal ort feasta;
Síneann do bhlaosc go dtí críocha na síoraíochta,
Mar a bhfuil an sú láidir ag brúchtaíl in airde.
Tagann loinnir ón dtaobh amuigh á ghríosadh,

Is anois beidh na grianta ar fad os do chionn
Ar dearglasadh, ar chúl a gcinn.
Ach laistigh díot féin tá dúil ag borradh
A mhairfidh tar éis grianta a bheith marbh id dhiaidh.

ó Ghearmáinis Rainer Maria Rilke

Buddha in Glory

Kernel of kernels, core of all cores,
An almond, self-contained and sweetening —
This universe, to the uttermost star,
Is your fruit and flesh: I send you greetings.

Now you know you are unencumbered;
Your shell has stretched into the infinite,
Where the vibrant sap rises and pulses.
An enabling light beams from a distance,

And now all of your suns will revolve,
Rich and glowing high overhead.
But something in you has begun to evolve,
That will live when all those suns are dead.

from the German of Rainer Maria Rilke

An Manach, na Lachain agus an Loch

Ní fhacas féin ach sraith ghriangrafanna,
Ach ó lámhchomharthaí an ghrianghrafadóra,
Maraon le cúpla focal a chompánaigh,
Thuigeas gurbh i bhfad i bhfad siar ó thuaidh
Ar Ardán na Tibeite lena 4x4 a bhíodar
Nuair a thángadar ar an manach is a scuaine,
É siúd go cúramach ag treorú lachan agus a h-ál
I dtreo locha bhí ina luí faoi bheanna sneachta;
Gur thuigeadar uaidh go raibh sé féin
I mbun oileathrachta fada sna críocha sin
Nuair a tháinig sé orthu, i bhfad ón uisce;
Go raibh sé tar éis a dhéanamh amach
Gur neadaigh an lacha tamaillín roimhe sin
Ar imeall an locha, ach de bharr athrú obann
Sa tséasúr, tuile nó tirimeacht éigin
A d'imigh thar tuiscint manach nó lacha,
Gur chúlaigh an loch i bhfad siar ón nead,
Agus nuair a rugadh an t-ál ar deireadh,
Nach raibh faic in aon chor ina dtimpeall
Ach cré leath-reoite, clochach. Dá bhrí sin,
Go raibh sé féin ag briseadh a oilithreachta
(D'fhéadfadh sé siúl níos tapiúla ina dhiaidh sin)
Is á mbeathú is a mealladh is á bpeataireacht
I dtreo an locha, mar nár mhaith leis
Roth a mbeatha a fheiscint ag imeacht i léig.

Rianaigh na grianghrafanna an scéal
Céim ar chéim go dtí gur shroicheadar
Ceann scríbe, agus gur sheas an manach
Faoi ghoirme spéir reoite an Earraigh
Ar bhruach locha a bhí chomh fairsing sin
Go sílfeá gur sheas sé ar bhruach an domhain.

The Monk, the Ducks and the Lake

I saw only a series of photographs,
But from the sign-language of the photographer,
Together with his friend's few words of English,
I made out it was in the far northwest part
Of the Tibetan plateau they were with their 4x4
When they came across this monk and his flock,
The monk carefully escorting a duck and her brood
Towards a lake under far, snow-clad summits;
That they had understood from him that he was
Undertaking a long pilgrimage through these parts
When he came across the ducks, far from water;
That he had concluded, after much thought,
That a duck and drake had nested some time before
At the lake's edge, but because of some change
Or other in the season, some drought or flood
Beyond the understanding of monks or ducks,
That the lake had retreated far from the nest
And when the now drakeless duck hatched the eggs
There was nothing at all visible around them
But stony, half-frozen clay. And so, he told them,
He was interrupting his pilgrimage for the time being
(He could always walk a little faster afterwards)
And feeding them and quacking them and coaxing them
Towards the lake, because he couldn't bear to see
The wheel of their small lives run down.

The photographs tracked the rest of the story
Step by waddling, guided step until they reached
Their destination, and the robed monk stood
Under the freezing blue sky of Spring
At the shore of a lake that stretched so far
You'd think he stood at the wide world's edge.

Agus cé na faca féin faic eile,
Tá tuairim agam gur leá criostal
I ndiaidh chriostail ghil oighir
Ar an sliabh, agus gur chromadar
Ag plimpeáil leo ceann ar cheann
Anuas sa mhullach ar a chéile
Ag sruthú leo i dtreo an locha;
Go raibh aoibh na n-aoibh ar an manach
Is é ag dordadh sútra ar an mbruach,
Ag guí leis na lachain ag lapadaíl sa láib,
Leis an roth ag rothaíocht ina cheart arís.

And although I saw or heard nothing else,
I have a notion that crystal
After crystal of shining ice melted
High up on the mountain, and began
Plinking and plinking one after another
Down on to another after another,
Gathering themselves towards the lake;
That the monk smiled as wide as the world
As he stood and droned a sutra on the shore,
Praying with the ducks' delighted dabbling,
With the wheel spinning at its own speed again.

Lótus Bhéarra

Is maith is cuimhin liom é,
An mhaidin aerach úd i mBéarra,
Spéir agus farraige fite fuaite
In aon ghealghoirme amháin,
Aiteann agus fraoch á mealladh isteach
I gcroithloinnir sin an chiúnais.

Is cuimhin liom an bóithrín casta
Go dtí an *Beara Dzogchen Retreat Centre*
A cheapfá a bheith díreach ar tí
Titim le faill, ach a dhein lúb obann
Aniar aduaidh ar féin agus timpeall
Ar linn sa bhfothain, niamhrach faoin ngréin.

Agus ansiúd ina lár, tá's ag Dia
Gan choinne ar domhan leis,
Bhí lótus corcra spréite romhainn,
Stróinséar blátha ón Domhan Toir,
Chomh cluthar sin go samhlófá é féin
Agus a sheacht shinnsear lótus roimhe
A bheith lonnaithe i lár na linne
Leis na cianta Béarracha.

Lótus sa linn,
Suíochán don Bhúda,
I measc fraoch agus aiteann Bhéarra,
An Búda sa linn, linn an Bhúda,
Dord na linne ag éirí ón lótus
Mar anál leoithneach,
Mar chumhracht oirthearach
In iarthar Bhéarra.

Lotus in Beara

It still breezes through my mind,
That airy morning in Beara,
The sea and the sky one
Seamless blue mantle,
Furze and heather seduced
Into that shimmering calm.

I remember the twisting boreen
To the Beara Dzogchen Retreat Centre,
That you'd think was about to
Topple over a cliff, but that turned
Back on itself out of the blue
Around a sheltered, sunlit pool.

And in the middle of the pool, God knows
Where on earth it blew in from,
A purple lotus spread itself under the sun,
A floral stranger from the East
Looking so snug that you'd imagine itself
And its seed, breed and generation
Had been settled in the pool
Since the time of the Flood.

A lotus in a pool,
A cushion for the Buddha
Among the heather and furze of Beara,
Buddha in the pool, the pool of Buddha,
The pool's prayer lilting through the lotus
In a breeze like a breath
Of eastern incense
On the western tip of Beara.

Sea is cuimhin liom an mhaidin
Aerach i mBéarra,
Is cuimhin liom an linn.

Yes, I remember that airy
Morning in Beara, and my mind still
Plunges deep in the pool.

The Alps of Chiang Mai

I wake to the grumbling of the fan,
The night outside throbbing with cicadas.

You are across in your narrow bed,
The streetlight catching the sheet

Draped over your humps and hollows
Like snow on mountains lit by stars.

I remember high meadows under snowy peaks
Where we crushed the scent from many flowers.

I will slip over under your sheet
And drench you with melting snow.

Step

It was a small miracle, the Buddha
Carved in a rock-face, gentling it
With outspread hands, robes flowing into petals.

Below, too sheer for trees, the mountain
Dropped away towards tiny villages
And terraced foothills leading to the city.

The others went ahead, following the ledge
That narrowed suddenly before it joined
A path that led to open, higher ground.

You're almost there, they coaxed, *just one more step
Is all*. Nothing on earth could make me face
The void that lay beyond that chiselled smile.

The Wind that Shakes the Barley

Small patches of barley settled themselves
Between the hills around the monastery,
And prayer-flags waved from the branches
That were stooked on every summit.

Yak-bells and the shouts of herding children
Were ringing along one valley or another
When the whole hillside suddenly exhaled
Trumpets, cymbals and the drone of scripture.

It was just a practice for the young monks
Shading themselves in the debate-garden,
Sometimes farting laughter into mouthpieces,
Their chants half joking, all in earnest,

As playfulness toyed with enlightenment,
And camera and cassette-recorder realised
Their inadequacy. Sutras droned territorially
As we made our way towards the mountain.

Later, we could see herds grazing the valleys,
The purple dots that were the monks' robes,
And, just about, hear the echoes of their trumpets,
While, far below, the soft wind shook the barley.

Layers

for Fang Yang Ying

When the huge Jade Dragon Snow Mountain
Hunched itself for days behind layers of cloud,
And hid its scaly peaks so that they gleamed
Only in half-remembered photographs,

I thought of those layered pagodas
Where a monk survives as a tiny crystal
That shines still behind the carved locks
Of stone doors that open only in the mind.

Bolgam

I gcúilsheomra sa mhainistir a bhíodar,
Dealbha gleoite snoite as im yeac,
Na dathanna ag brú a chéile chun solais
Nuair a chuardaigh an ghrian an seomra.

Caomhnaithe le luibheanna is spíosraí,
Mhairfidís deich mbliain sa dorchadas
Go dtí go ngabhfaidís slí na fírinne
Mar sholáthar turais do oilithrigh.

Bhí dragúin ag lúbadh trína chéile
Le sceitimíní ag lútáil leis an mBúda
A bhí ina shuí croschosach ar an lótas,
Aoibh shíoraí air faoi ór a chaidhpe.

Ar spraoi i measc bláthanna rábacha,
Bhí bandia cíochnocht ag seinm siotáir
Faoi mar a bheadh sí á méarú féin
Chun aoibhnis a leáfadh an t-im.

Le boladh géar an ime sa timpeall,
Smaoiníos ar Imbolc, is ar bha draíochta
A thál bainne gan stad ar fhocal naoimh,
Is dheineas aon bholgam amháin den domhan.

Shamhlaíos fallaing mhíorúilteach Bhríd
Ag leathnú de shíor thar shléibhte soir,
Agus im míorúilteach sin an Oirthir
Ag brúchtaíl thar mhachairí uile Chill Dara.

Gulp

They were in a back room of the monastery,
Exquisite figures sculpted in yak butter,
Their colours pushing one another towards the light
As the sun searched through the dusty room.

Preserved with ritual herbs and spices,
They would live in darkness for ten years
Before undertaking a sacred journey
As food in the bags of pilgrims.

Dragons twisted and twined themselves
In fawning ecstasy around the Buddha
Who sat cross-legged on a lotus blossom
Smiling eternally below his golden hood.

Surrounded by a riot of flowers,
A bare-breasted goddess played a sitar
As though she were fingering herself
Towards a pleasure to make her melt.

With the tang of the butter in the air,
I thought of *Imbolc*, and of magic cows
That yielded endless milk on a saint's word.
And I swallowed the whole world at one gulp.

I imagined Saint Brigid's miraculous cloak
Spreading seamlessly eastward over the Himalya,
And a sea of pungent, miraculous butter
Overflowing westward to the plains of Kildare.

Tibetan Shepherd Boys

It was all true, everything you'd read,
The open faces, the wide-eyed delight
In stroking the hairs of my arms,
The infectious, endless laughing.

It was wonderful, too, the agility
As they raced away after sheep,
Waving from high, dizzy paths,
Their goodbyes bouncing between cliffs.

And I could see, from a distance,
The incredible speed and grace they showed
As they cut out and caught a wild goat
And kicked and stoned him, just for the hell of it.

Kho Samet

The coral on the reef
Is brain and lung pulsing,
Forming and endlessly reforming
Flowers into stone.

Between the urchins' spikes,
Patterns of iridescent circles
Are glittering like stars
Frightened of immensities.

Above the beach, the trees
Bud and blossom and wither
At one and the same time,
And know no seasons.

Ag an Droichead a Cruthaíodh ar Neamh

Tá mar a bheadh loirg cos brúite anseo san aolchloch,
Paidreacha greanta ar leaca, agus cuimhne ag an gcarraig
Ar scéal scéil faoi thuras go dtí an Domhan Thiar
D'fhonn eagna Bhúda a bhreith abhaile ón Ind.

Thar teorainn anseo a thángadar, na h-oilithrigh,
Ag cuartú na dtrí ciseán, Dlí, Agallamh agus Scrioptúr,
Is athnuachan ar smior na gcnámh, ar fhuil na feola:
Manach i mbláth a aithbhreithe, muc glic, agus rógaire moncaí

A chothaigh, de bharr daonnacht a dhéithiúileachta,
Agus ainmhíocht neamhthruaillithe a dhaonnachta,
Raic i bPálás Neimhe, iontas ar Shealúchas an Chré,
Agus borradh nua in Impireacht na Marbh.

Ag an droichead Neamhdhéanta seo idir dhá ríocht,
D'fhág gach aon deamhan is drochrud is dragún
A bhí á gciapadh go dtí sin, faoiseamh acu ar deireadh,
Agus ghluaiseadar le leoithne cumhra trí úllghoirt fairsinge.

Teanntaithe idir failltreacha, tá an abhainn
Ina tuile buí ag réabadh thar charraigreacha,
Agus uisce ón lochán gaile lena h-ais
Ag beiriú ón dtalamh trínachéile laistíos.

Tá an áirse ollmhór cloiche os ár gcionn
Ag fáisceadh na bhfailltreacha lena chéile,
Is ag rá: *Ní bheifear scartha. In ainneoin teorainneacha,*
A thaistealaithe, tá sibh i gcríocha na droicheadúileachta

At the Bridge Made in Heaven

Here are footprints of legend in the limestone,
Prayers carved on slabs, the rock still remembering
The tale told of a journey to the Western World
To bring back from India the wisdom of the Buddha.

Here they crossed borders, those pilgrims who sought
The three baskets of Law, Dialogue and Scripture
And renewal of the bone's marrow, the flesh's blood:
A reincarnated monk, a sly pig and a wise rogue of a monkey

Whose constant shifting between the humanity of his divinity
And the unadulterated simianism of his humanity,
Caused uproar in Heaven, amazement on Earth,
And fresh stirrings in the Kingdom of the Dead.

Here at this Heaven-made bridge between kingdoms,
Those devils, dragons and other damnable beings
Who had tormented them, left them at last
To travel in peace through fragrant orchards.

Confined between canyon walls, the river
Is a yellow flood thundering over boulders,
While the water in the thermal pool close by
Steams and bubbles with subterranean agitation.

The huge arch of rock stretching overhead
Spans the canyon, squeezing its walls together,
Saying: *There will be no severance. In spite of borders,*
Travellers, you have arrived in the realm of bridges.

Umbrellas, Xiahe

On one peak among many,
High above the monastery,
Two monks in purple robes
Spread a picnic before them.

In the thin, burning air,
Umbrellas, one red, one blue,
Over small pools of shade
Seem ready to float away

As the monks rise and settle,
Turn and turn about
According to the sun.
Monet might have travelled

To see the two hemispheres
Shimmer into the still
Spinning *yin* and *yang*,
Of each and of other.

Guided Tour, Xiahe

Long ago, he explained, *for many monk*
The meditation was only in the cave.
And in the cave, he does not eat, only
Flowers from the garden and the grasslands.

He smiled, and moved to the next painting.
In the pause between, I could feel
The darkness blossoming, the dank air sweetening,
And petals falling lightly through my mind.

Corra Bána
do Éanna

Bhí sé beagnach dearmadta agam, an crann sin
A chonac ón mbus, taobh amuigh de bhaile,
É breac le corra bána suite mar a bheadh éarlais
Ar ghrástúlacht, fad saoil agus bheith ann don eile.

Fad saoil chugat féin, mar sin, a rug abhaile
Ód chuid taistil féin an bhratóg síoda,
Deartha leis na héin rathúla chéanna
A thuirling im aigne le cleitearnach aoibhinn.

Agus tá siad neadaithe i gcónaí faram,
Ag saibhriú an tseomra le cumhracht na Síne,
Suite gan bhogadh ar ghiúis is ar charraig.
Is nuair a chraitheann an bhratóg i bpuithín gaoithe,

Cloisim, ar feadh soicind, mionabhar na síoraíochta
Sa leoithne éadrom ag siosarnach trín síoda.

White Cranes
for Éanna

It had almost slipped my mind, that tree
I had glimpsed once from a trundling bus,
Dappled with cranes like long-standing promises
Of grace, long life and the truth of otherness.

So long life to you too, for bringing home
From your own travels, this painted silk
Bright with those same auspicious birds,
To land in my mind on exhilarated wings.

They are nesting still on my sitting-room wall,
Endowing the room with wealth from the east,
Perched now for good on rocks among pine-trees,
And when the scroll stirs in a sudden breeze,

I hear for a moment in that passing wind
Murmurs of eternity rustling through the silk.

Na Trí Phagóda, Dali

Sa tSínis, ní bhíonn aon aimsir
Ag an mbriathar. Bíonn gach
A bhfuil, a bhí agus a bheidh
Láithreach ar an aon fhocal.

Chuimhníos ar sin nuair a chonac
Na trí phagóda atá ag dreapadh
Céim ar chéim le míle bliain
Go ciúin i dtreo scamall na sléibhte,

Agus ag tomadh céim ar chéim
Ag an am gcéanna síos díreach
I dtreo chlúmh na scamall céanna
I scathán an locha lena n-ais.

Is dob é saoi na saoithe a leomhfadh a rá
Cá bhfaighfí teacht ar iomláine a dtógála.

The Three Pagodas, Dali

In Mandarin, the verb recognises
No tenses. Everything that is,
That was and that will be, becomes
Present and correct in the one word.

I remembered that much when I saw
The three great pagodas still climbing
After a thousand years, layer after layer,
Towards clouded mountain summits,

And plunging, layer after layer,
At the same time straight down
Again towards those clouded summits
In the nearby lake's reflection.

Only the sage of all sages would dare
To guess at their points of completion.

Archaeological Site, Kyongu

In the surrounding fields
Hunched figures moving slowly,
Coaxing the year's crop.

Inside roped-off plots
Workers scraping and rooting
For fragments of dynasty.

At a nearby roundabout
Hyundai trucks belching smoke,
Roaring like disturbed dragons.

And overhead, the elegant hauteur
Of a long flight of cranes
Instinctively sure of lineage.

Three

Ritual for the Propitiation
of the Abnormal Dead

Among the Naxi, the Dongba priests,
With flags and images, grain and eggs,
Build a Village of the Abnormal Dead
Where the wandering spirits of those who died
By murder, suicide and war are danced
Into quietude, their village gently destroyed.

I would have them dance all over Ireland,
In towns and villages, and along ditches
Where bodies have been found, and not found.
I would have them dance in Greysteel and in Omagh,
In Monaghan, Soloheadbeg and Kilmainham.
I would have them dance in Enniskillen, Béal na Bláth,
In Ravensdale and Ballyseedy, Talbot Street and Warrenpoint.

I would have them dance every bloody sunday
And weekday until only the everyday
Spirits are abroad for their allotted time,
Before they rest, and let the living live.

Squirrels

They were being sold as pets, it was explained,
As the two squirrels spun and spun in a cage
At a street-market where the Great Wall
Continued its imperial declaration,
Like a dragon hauling its wounded bulk
From ridge to wooded ridge above us.

I remembered a temple among trees
Where a squirrel cocked its head at me
Then spiralled up a trunk and flashed
From branch to bending branch, then floated
Dreamily with paws and tail stretched out
To land on the tiled roof of the temple

As lightly as a question springs to mind
Or an acorn settles among dead leaves.

In the Summer Palace
for Hu Xiang Qun

Towards the century's turn, the Dowager Empress
With courtiers and attendant eunuchs promenades
Across the seventeen perfectly spaced arches
Of a sun-dazed bridge, between summer rains.

Shaded by parasols and willow branches,
They scatter crumbs among carp and goldfish,
Discovering constantly new perspectives
Westward, towards The Fragrant Hills.

Along the great bends of the Yangtse,
The yellow, eroded clay collapses
Inexorably into landslides,
And oozes towards the swollen river

That will burst its banks again this year
As the scarred, exhausted mountains
Steel themselves against the rain
And ache for their forest roots.

They pass the Hall of Literary Prosperity,
Where, delicately, for fear of damage,
Scholars in silk robes unwind scrolls,
Calligraphing the art of government.

Outside, an ox cast in bronze
Chews the cud of many centuries,
Her placid reflection in the lake
A totem against threatened floods.

All across the provinces, dragons blink
To find themselves pulling railway cars,
While words like imperial *and* dynasty
Are striking a different note in the streets.

In the stinking alleys, in the lecture-halls,
In villages along the terraced hills,
Ideas throb like cicadas, sing like caged birds
And flow like endless cups in teahouses.

Along the colonnade of the Long Corridor,
They admire painting after exquisite painting
Of myth and dynasty and history
That lead them to a pavilion by a pond,

Where, soothed by their peacock-feather fans,
And schooled to trace the music in a poem,
The courtiers sit and pattern the sound
Of raindrops falling on the lotus leaves.

Models

Mao played a minor role in the First Congress
Philip Short, *Mao: a life*

The museum on the site of the first
Congress Of The Chinese Communist Party
Is reconstructed in the old colonial style.
All of the doorways are granite.

In a wax model, Mao, illuminated
By hindsight, stands and gesticulates.
The lighting is hidden, so that the glow
On his face seems interior, visionary.

The other twelve delegates, just one
Of whom will survive into government,
Hang on every word. They do not notice
The tea-boy who glides between them.

All of the delegates are identified,
Their names engraved near ghostly figures
On a metal plaque. Only the tea-boy,
Who is not listening, remains anonymous.

Éin i gCliabháin

Ar fhalla íseal cois fuaráin
I measc na gcrann a chonac iad,
Stocaireacht na tráchta á dtimpeallú
Ar oileán in aigéan rachmais.

Thángadar ann le maidí siúil
Gach aon mhaidin, ag tarraingt na gcos,
Ag iompar leo a gcuid éiníní cheoil
I gcliabháin ornáideacha bambú.

Meigill mhandairíneacha orthu
Faoina gcuid caipíní Maoacha,
Toitín ag sileadh le gach aon bhéal,
Bhlaiseadar de chiúnas na seanaoise.

Agus lean an trácht leis á dtimpeallú,
Na héin i gcliabháin, na seanfhondúirí.

Caged Birds

They sat on a low stone wall
By a fountain among the trees,
The blare of traffic surrounding
That island in a sea of affluence.

They came with their sticks
Every morning, dragging their feet,
Carrying their songbirds
In ornate bamboo cages.

They had Mandarin goatees
Below their Mao caps.
Cigarettes drooping from their mouths,
They inhaled the silence of their age.

And the traffic surged non-stop around them,
The caged birds, the old brigade.

At the Village of the Stone Drum

Shigu. The Stone Drum. On terraced hills
Above the first bend of the Yangtze
The inscription on the great stone wheel
Booms out, across five centuries,

Victory! History! Dynasty! On a nearby hill,
Two heroic figures, soldier and peasant,
Clasp eager hands in sculpted memory
Of a river crossed, a retreat transformed.

They are not listening to the drum. They strain
In every sinew towards the end of dynasties.
It is the Long March and the soldier will cross
The Yangtze, and the peasant will help him, and wait.

Their gaze is locked, each in the other,
In a bronze pleading, and a bronze promise,
That the marchers will return across terraces,
Will climb over walls, will scale the dragon's back.

In their eyes too, perhaps, a bronze despair, knowing
That rhythm can be lost in its own hammering,
And the dancing words of a new anthem can stiffen
Into proclamations chiselled on a stone drum.

The Master Calligrapher

He moves easily between styles, absorbing
The character of the times as quickly
As his brush soaks ink. A few strokes
For example, fill the great square
With thousands of faces in an urgent,
Open-ended style, the characters
Simply formed and full of exuberance.

He is equally a master of the older
Clerical script favoured for decrees,
Whose closed and unambiguous characters
Move in unison to surround the square
As marching feet or the tracks of tanks.
Brush poised, he contemplates the final
Balance his manuscript must achieve.

These are the broad strokes. The detail
Is where his controlling genius shows.
Connoisseurs will notice, for example,
How his rendering of the man hidden
Behind screens in the state apartments
Echoes the ideograph of the young man
With arms spread in the path of a tank.

They will notice that the passionate strokes
Delineating the young man's stance and words
Are repeated in a more rigid form to convey
The unheard words and hidden gestures of the other.
They will notice that this subtle change of emphasis
Tightens those outspread arms to a resigned shrug,
And turns a manifesto into a brusque command.

The Paving Stones of Tiananmen Square

They have laid down new paving on Tiananmen Square,
Small armies ceaselessly levelling and barrowing
Along dusty paths and trenches, sweating by day
Under a sun that quivered like a gong, by night
Changing shift for exhausted shift, snatching
A quick smoke near the floodlit, chain-wire fence.

The blank verse of the five great arches,
Below the genial portrait, anticipates
The marching feet, the trundling tanks
 That will proclaim the anniversary
Whose stately and implacable rhythms echo
Across the measured paving stones by day.

The lyrical, on the other hand, comes out by night
And strolls among the families around the square,
Where fluttering kites blossom like flowers
And a hundred strings contend for space,
Inching towards a level where butterflies and dragons
Can soar above stones that are smooth and unstained.

July 1999.